BLUE MAGIC

~A PRELUDE TO LOVE~

Collection of Poetry

By Ms. Jessica Hughes

I

ISBN 13: 978-0692359808

First Printing, 2014

CreateSpace Publishing Co.

The Woman Behind The Words

Ms. Jessica Hughes better known as Jhpoetry in the cyber world has been writing for more than ten years. She was born and raised in the upper parts of South Carolina. As the only child to a single parent she became creative early in life. And this imaginative seed grew well into her adulthood where she fell in love with her muse. During this time span, Jessica has used the tool of poetry to express her voice. And in doing so she has been widely noted as a diverse poetess. However, Ms. Jessica's new collection of poems "BLUE MAGIC " ~ A Prelude To Love~ is a scope into the rebirth of her most intimate works. Her sensual intrigues, spiritual sway and romantic passages invite the reader into her own world of magic. This is where she draws you under her spell with potent words, vibrant metaphors that prepare a feast for those who wish to partake in the bliss of love. Still, there is more for the reader to be ecstatic about. The "BLUE MAGIC" edition will continue to be penned in the spirit of romance in upcoming years by non-other than the Poetess herself.

Reviews

Jessica's poetry is a pleasure to read, she manages to unmask but still leave intrigue in each scribe. – Vic Emerson

I have been reading Jh's poetry for quite some time and I always come away very moved by elicited emotion. With delicate, yet strong visuals throughout, Jessica does a simply beautiful job in working her poetical tapestries. She utilizes her tremendous talent with the gift of word. – Deborah L. Kelly

BLUE MAGIC

~ A PRELUDE TO LOVE~

Collection of Poetry

By Ms. Jessica Hughes

IV

Quotes and Inspirations

Romance is set apart from all other forms of love
by the intensity of bliss.
Bliss is natural to life, but once we cover it over,
we must search for it in others.
The pain of yearning is a mask for the ecstasy of bliss.
Bliss is not a feeling but a state of being.
In the state of bliss, everything is loved.

-Deepak Chopra

V

"My mission in life is not merely to survive, but to thrive; and to do so with some passion, some compassion, some humor, and some style."

-Maya Angelou

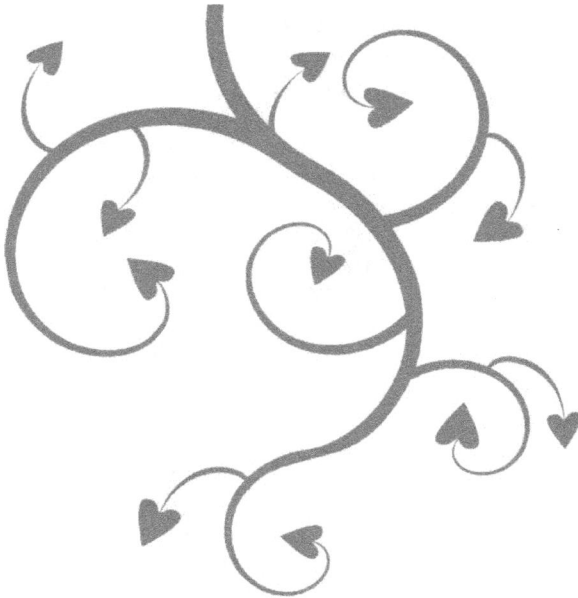

"My love feeds on your love beloved, and as long as you live it will be in your arms without leaving mine."

- Pablo Neruda

VI

Table of Contents

Secret Admirer

My secret admirer, we rendezvous at twilight.
We undress the trivial pseudos' while pursing in the matrix of
our deities. You weep at the mortal soul especially those
whom prostitute love into pigeon holes...
They suffocate its meaning.

We are alive- fertile specimens enriching as Alpha in every
season. There is none equal to the capabilities we've shown
one another.

We are as tall as the Redwood trees within Cupid's garden.
I ask you to listen to the arcane rivers as we fish in fresh water
lakes. Inhale the winds purr along the ocean's wave of
speechless words.

Sit with me my admirer just before the stars blink goodnight.
Time is on our side. It is a young Zion for us to implore.

And quietly, we peer into tomorrow's promise. As our soar of
compassion inspire to converge like nestled birds.
We trace and flatter the spawning fabric of our seeking hearts.

The Muse of Me

I am mesmerized by you.
As the days turn to months and months to years;
your persistent love for me and I for you follows.
A friendship turned to love, that sparked a passion from a
flame. It burns eternal in my dwellings. I have no crown; yet
you placed laurels upon my head, crowning you the muse of
me. The goddesses of Zeus worked magic within my mind,
and zapped my fingers with a magic wand. The rivers of ink
have flowed ever since. I am obsessed in your everlasting
springtime. This is a beautiful crazy if any one beholds thee.
We complement one another. We know our thoughts and how
to create the perfect work of us. I contemplate with grief if I
ever loss your precious gift. Time would be a waste. Life
would be a meaningless existence. My meditation is focused
on our impulsive sessions. Forever we shall be entwined as
lovers in rhapsody. The muse of me__

2

The Lonely Affair

In thunder roaring nights; the flame flickers
There is sparkle upon your skin. I see.
As the tremble inside consummates romance.
There is red in you. There is brighter red in me.
The shadows glaze us a striped candy cane.
Beat for us. Beat more stripes until it glows...
Night sticks that quiver in the dark...
We roll together within intimate blaze.
The color of dawn is in your eyes.
As they draw us into a lonely affair.
The flame flickers.
The stripes beat more and more.
And quietly we rain the night until
our souls become a storm.
Grasping the hostage of inward affection
in our lonely affair.
We flicker. We tremble. We quiver.
The red in you licks a brighter red in me.
In thunder roaring nights, I see eyes of flame.

3

Walking In The Night

Boldly, we walk in a shadow,
unafraid of the figurines before sunset,
and the flock of crows whom fly into darkness,
as our legs intertwine on riveting roads,
we walk into the glittering shadows,
ignoring the yen of the dead,
flaunting the newness of love's subtle touch,
finding the refuge of forever yours upon a face,
who should forget? who should fret sunsets
upon each dawning footstep?
what a harvest of emotion on this quiet eve,
the world shall not bare such happiness; the sea shall
not bellow its tranquil sound in another's home,
now, the clock pauses at the hint of your sweetness,
the black bird no longer answers my reason,
for the atmosphere has secured our true silhouettes,
tomorrow would be too soon to forget

A Prominent Love

Good morning love, his voice ladybugs out to thee
Magically, he sooths my aspen fears; the ones that appear like
dragon flies between flashes of light.

And then, the lure of his physique approaches mine.
Intensely, I brush my hair. For a mistress must be prepared for
her groom.

I tell him to meet me soon at the golden bridge and judge not
the darkest hours inside hidden skies.
But, measure his faith where our treasure lies_

Evening shines upon warm torches leaning side by side in
courtesy.

We forgive ourselves to uncover a wealth of waterfalls.
As the day grows small, relief from tears savor our marriage
bed-

We are silent; we wheeze, gasp and breathe as I kiss his
forehead good night and fall gently asleep.

Bad Drug

I'm the fixer
The elixir of any pain
You comely thing
Lay those burdens
In a lap of insane
Tap dancing
On each and every membrane
That's what I do
When there is no cure

Sniff my hair, inhale my beauty
Inject yourself wherever
It feels genuine
I'll wait as always
For her withdrawals
For her rejection
She under appreciates
What I value
What a pity

Nowhere

Nowhere remove thou love
Nowhere as distant miles afar
Stay close as the blood in my veins
A constant recycle of why I live. What I'm living for....

For I may go paranoid and declare me mental
Spineless I am when your strong scent I sniffle
As it flourishes and bounce; close to you is my house

There, making you my man with gentle caress of hands
That cause the ground to blush; nature smiles upon our crush
As we enthrall in one another's self: producing the selfless
love

And my dream is there___ inside of you and you inside of me
The way life was intended to grow inward and bloom outward
As spring flowers: as poetry that ignites and consume

Nowhere fulfill another lust
Nowhere find yourself losing us
My heart may burst from the pain
If that be, love cannot sustain
Even to return in remained regret
Therefore, nowhere remove thou self

Paridiso Esta Aqui

At last, the yearning pains shall dock,
As passing ships pursue the dreamy light house,
No longer lost at sea or sailing solo in crashing waves,
The day is young as the baby crabs, juicy oysters
and sea shells that whisper "paridiso esta aqui" ,
feelings begin to burn like firewater- bubbling over,
intimate thoughts adrift into physical sunrise ,
for passions have arrived, as bumps rock the boat,
romance is a floating petal, engulfing in high tide ,
orchestrating the zest for love, our flood drips from,
the mouth of the ocean, our pungent smell awakens,
the gyrating land as steamboats perfume the sky.

8

Lying Here

I allude back to my luminous morning. He was the one who inspired me to slow dance with poetry. At first I rebelled against my feelings, the thought of I and poetry engaged in such an act left a pondering.

For poetry is a universal language only the rarest of the rare can transcend... But, as he spilled from his soul, my closed heart began to open to him. My pen began to wiggle into the deepness of this divine expression.

And then he left like a fleeting ghost. This is when I became the lonely poet. Days could go by and I would visualize his orchid lips that caressed my insecure inkwell. In the noon day, I'd spend hours feeding on the substance I held dearly... warm sunrises, my sounding pulse and dwelling on his enticing words.

Every day my pen would feather. Every day I would become fonder of the man who freed these lips of mind. Nowadays, the wind blows a little softer under my chin. Intimacy sits a little longer as I girdle my love story. The tassel upon my brow wakens the goddess of writing. And he pianos right beside me as I lose myself within a lucid light of Poetry~`

A Complicated Thing

Fate had us from the start
You and I spin in the center of nature's turmoil
Lost and found in grey storms
Both twirling hand in hand in wind's gust
Playing without a care in our own dirt
Until time's painful tares began to hurt
_In the pit of night's stomach
I'll be the advocate, dismissing our tears
Nurturing what survives among the years
And the nervous wind blows still, shrugging
As we stare at the best direction to go
Breaching what society deems wrong
In us I can find none

10

My Twilight

In the twilight, rhapsody calls
the waning candle in a fawning ear
bathing in exotic bath oils, prim and proper
I sit shimmering in diffusion
which summons a warm caress
one that kisses me inside and moves me around
like the stars parting in the sky,
happiness is dawning, happiness is dawning,
a rising and falling beauty, poetry in motion
an orange vibration doing the morning rumba
and it coils and squeezes when we eclipse
I hold on, I hold on for dear life

11

.

In Your Solitude

Can we share comforting solitude under a country shed?
I like to go there when it rains to hear the drizzle upon a tin
roof. There, I have been in slumber. But, if you sit with me, I
would have more to offer.

Here, I hold a hat made of woven fabric,
it hovers the chilly days and nights. However, a fire would
ignite without furnace or fireplace when your skin brushes my
skin, stirring beautiful wildfires into my soul.

The day is sunny and the birds are flying south.
In restless solitude I pine beside the pecan tree.
The tree is going bare for season has changed
.
Today, I flopped among a small patch of grass and imagined
you beside me.

I hear the rustling in the woods where a worn walk has been
made into a muddy pathway. As I close my eyes, the taste of
your breath brings me out of boredom.

Then I don't feel alone. I grin; laugh a little each time you and I
meet. Until, the path is clear and your face disappears.

No Strings

Pieces of thread cling from polyester sweaters,
old letters snowflake a quilted mattress,
memories erupt as the fountains in Time Square,
bringing feelings back alive,
as neon street signs begin to come on,
the cooling sun deepens the tone,
bright eyes are focused on a fixated passion,
In the background curling toes,
spiral into soft melody,
And behind those almond blinds,
misty talk and cashew promises greet,
like footprints on hot pavement
A wet kiss here- a nice rub there -
should ease this muscle tension.

13

Only Love

Many seek the finer yet, I yearn to possess
the most precious asset called Love.

For what is my true purpose in longing without
beholding Love.

It does outweigh the heaviest bars of gold.
As thy shimmer set a sight before thee.

Beyond a clear sunrise and peaking sunset I see the vision.
The feel of something special emerging in your lions.
A soft and tranquil music.

And the ticking organ amongst our chest walls sustains us.
Still, it cannot maintain our mortal souls eternal.
On the day of our departure, these gentle winds shall stir the
sands. And the heat shall burn like the sun of life.

It shall chamber like the hour glass.
It shall last until the energies meet in time.
For the continuous pours of sand are endless.

Patience has a say, it will not be in vain as the scorned harlot.
My thoughts will not be shallow as those whom try and taint
Love. For someday the truth shall bathe in the ocean's depth.

I'll sow you.
I'll harvest you.
I'll take good care of you.

Only Love cont'd

If you can hear my whisper mingling in space than stare the
moon into my embrace.

I'll be here until a season beckons unto another season.
Come and be filled with my merriment.
And I shall grip you with an iron fist.

Befitting

When the red carpet is folded, tucked inside the heir's rightful garment, there will come a time for a true unveiling of the original crown royal. Like the prestigious stars that are star struck in the limelight, our stomachs shall digest them in the pool of tainted blood lines. They shall be loosed like golden coins, flying in the gusty wind. Unlike others who jester at the mere ideology of a loyal companionship; they judge us as nothing more than poor men and women. However, in our minds we are rich… we are richer than the mediocre spirit. Ultimately, we negotiate how to explain this pious act to the masses. But then, decide actions should speak for themselves. For class is insignificant without pupils. For our devoted love is well polished and refined before the whistling of the chime. And then we must listen- so not to fret as the gates of hell would not survive what we have conquered.

Befitting cont'd

Our soul given character is most important.

Like a china vase holding moral fibers. We are equally yoked,

never cracking at the boiling points.

Still, outsiders and negative forces continue to wage war.

But, we need not beat against the air.

Therefore, this process takes initiative when our positions

become Crown Realized.

17

The Rain Speaks

Every day the rain speaks to me.
During tender moments I watch full moon eyes.
I see hands that gently massage me like a love song.
Sometimes I'm ashamed, afraid of the happiness.
I've been in the rain. It has brought misery to me.
It has brought comfort as well.
For once, my soul peacefully slumbers and my missing
half has been woven whole. As my purest form of hope
lingers in the rain, I have faith on a gloomy day.
It leaps around the obvious I use to ignore.

The Beauty of Him

There is comeliness in a man's smile; the noble peace prize in his eyes like the orange glow of sunrise--

He is ken, yet humble as the house upon prairie hills. Being the man whom coincides with his dreams,

sacrificing bits of himself to those denied, kissing his lady with adoring pride. Should he ever walk into my life, instantly, I would recognize him.

And his affections I would not shun, but relish them all year long. He is a gem; a hard to be found meekness in fanciful imagery.

Still he is out there producing his destiny, respectfully meeting his goals and inspiring others.

He is a gentleman to any mother, sister or daughter. He is the difference between boy and man. For his discipline is made of kind hands.

Whether he loses or gains, his composure remains the same. He is a man who seeks truth in every deed. He is the man whose heart was meant to bleed.

He is the source of tantalizing elation. The beauty of him is the rarest of our divine creations.

Night of Love

O' lovely night, serene and crisp
Follow the moon full to its lead
Hear the wolves howl for him
The acute wanders in my heart

Send him urgent before I change
From the shreds of breathless borrowed
May he grace me gorgeous
His flower of precious burnings

O' lovely night, the stars sparkle brighter
It bellows our song betwixt lyrics spring
As dewy ears repose to a beckoning bloom
There the chanting of soprano whispers

As our sound bound us found
As our sound be loose forever
As we high pitch in desire always

Summer In Winter

I have felt summer in winter.
Right by the camp fire there is serenest and
alluring gestures that melt the ice.
The hints of summer blush about.
A whirlwind of snow captures our sultry sprawls,
fervid silhouettes and star searching through the night.
We have become the white hot heat; the winters hottest
tremble. Clothes off are on nothing can stop this blue passion.
In your eyes burns my eternal candle.
You can blow on my fingertips;
I shall kiss the bite from your lips.
As our bodies swell over and over.
On this aching night everything is burning, sweating and
making winter sigh.

Maple Syrup

small back aches accommodate
hoarse vocals at daybreak

a strand of dread lock
a pinky finger nail
falls against black tattoos

firm buttocks , jiggle
persuasive comments ride
into morning traffic

she fakes possum
he strokes his ego
beside a fluffy pancake

brown sugar and maple syrup
spread eagle at each corner
sweet and sticky

flip,flop, and apple turnovers
listening to the humming AC unit
a greasy tablecloth gives in
tangible has its advantages

22

So Few

There are so few...
Men who enjoy a little sweat
From oil changes, fixing flats,
Or slaving over a hot stove,
Musty odors trailing the corridors
Begging him to hit the showers
Very few, hold on to chivalry
Protecting their manhood,
Walking side by side with the lady of their dreams,
earning a honest living
Knowing how to care for his wife and
Not easily persuaded by his lazy eye
He's doesn't fall prey to the new
"Millennium Style"
He savors a strong reflection
Watching himself in her perfections
Staying in love with her revered intellect
Appreciating her intimacy outside of bed

"Give him a plaque."
"No, he deserves a hand clap."

But, what he longs for is a pat
on the back.

She Is Adored

When the dirt stirred and transformed her skin, she was precious beauty in the makings.

She titles Mother Earth, dipping her temple in pure water-- gorgeous flowers sailing around, for she is dedicated to the duties that are bound to be.

The nurturer, wiping tears away, the giver whom works more but, receives less pay.

Still, her graceful strength ensues like a melodious flow. Her heart is captured in gold. Her soul renews the old.

And the love she continuously blooms like the rose in June. People often wonder how much sunshine can be born to a woman in the misty rain.

Therefore, she understands her commands as she reflects good upon herself: husband, children and friends.

She is the Queen of the Nile; the neighbor next door. May we all be thankful in her presence for she is adored.

Irresistible

Through his windows, I can conceive a beautiful spirit.
He touches me with nerve, where others
may pursue but never reach.
As I gaze into his window, the light is blinding for all to see.
I am so lucky to be amid his aura.
Yet, he gazes at me with a humble heart.
Am I his? Have we found our forever?
Instantly, I fall deep into his arms.
His arms are strong enough to cradle me.
I will rock for days on days, wherever he lies.
My one wish is to be close to him.
He mysteriously captures me from everyone
and everything.

25

Charmed

Your lips move

weightless as a light breeze

words that are heavy

as my sweaty palms

ravishing in anticipation

I pace, your face opens

my portals soak

in small truths

truths that season my bland

growing in my head

growing in my heart

in the corners of a vacant room

making me greedy

making me tasty

as a honey melon

Bud

Love has bared its unadulterated conscious; the acquitted
bud.

Tonight, bodies waver in moon bathing tide. The undertones
of adduced flesh lisp a raspberry sap.

I'm relaxed, mushed within your sanctity as I become the
aphrodisiac which pleases your kissing cherub.

Lying next to your pronounced muscle, the flush of heat
intensely arouses within me. My urge is cage free, spilling
over, sweating pores as a Niagara Falls.

Temptation is beautiful. More beautiful than crisp autumn
colors on leafs. Even the bending candles are swaying me to
flame this ember.

I must toss my bouquet of chaste to the maidens.
I must sample the hunger inside. And feel how deep the water
rises. Taste the pineapple; I'm sure will tingle my bones.

Exfoliate my interior into a vulnerable creature.
For we pedaled in pure ecstasy and it should reflect as such.

Blue Magic

Who would of thought, a slight midnight
shade of blue would work me,
impress upon my mind his chiseled features.
He seemed all about businesses.
I was kind of disappointed he didn't flirt with me.
It was obvious I wasn't interested in what he
was selling, I could buy a slab of bologna at the store.
The whiff of his cheap musk ignited my allergies.
I sucked in a deep one like pulling on my last cigarette.
The inhale gave me a high I would never forget.
My long, mature arms yearend to touch his fresh from
"The consignment shop suit." I was a woman with class.
Therefore, I ignored his dashing attempt to overdo it.
However, his pinstriped suit was a serious attention getter.
I didn't mind; it made his 5"5 frame climb a bit closer to mine.

Blue Magic (A Prelude to Love)

You must understand I heard a mystery in his voice.
A firm yet sensitive demeanor as he looked directly into my
spirit. Inadvertently, I turned my head from his overwhelming
presence. I wanted to fly, I had wings... the angles had finally
answered my prayers. This is what I felt... The sex goddess
must have given me her strength. My rivers were flowing,
feeling light headed from imagined ecstasy. I had thrown
chastity to the wind. And then his discussion was done but,
the inevitable had begun. As we shook on it, the earth shifted
in our favor. The heat rose in between our space. The one we
would explore at the right time and place. When the stars
aligned with the moon that is when he would cause me to
scream to the heavens.

28

Can't Get Enough

This morning I fought hard with myself, knocking my head upside the headboard, beating my fist against the Chester drawer. I'd say our fight was a draw. There were no knockouts or referees. But, believe me when I say we both threw in the towel after 2:00 a.m. The flashes of fury I couldn't bear to entertain any longer. In silence, I washed the salted crust from my cheek. I had become delusional; I swore in every room I heard your heavy breaths. Instead of strong black coffee stains, the kitchen counter was glossed in your beads of sweat. It hadn't been 24 hours; yet, I wanted to report you missing… The house was too empty without our mumblings. I needed to hear our funky rumbling, the special spot we had in common. You loved making things up to me. And I loved giving it to you. No, I wouldn't rest until I heard that funky music banging inside my walls. I wouldn't call it quits until I heard the neighbors holla OMG!

29

The Way You Love

You have a way of catching me off guard.
I've tried to avoid you and it. I cannot lie.
My hands are tied in your soft leather and
succulent touch, well...
It's simply is a tough resistance.
Your eyes tell me to put away the key.
You won't me to stay for eternity.
How can I not love you?
My pulse beats on every occasion.
The sigh in our noon day connection;
A rainbow of assorted affections.
How can I not love you?
I'm the writer and you're the book.
We are one in the same, still learning and
gaining in our wisdoms. Your heart drips
and I listen~~ as I lend my ear unto
a greater cause. To enjoy what exist
between the oceans deep and mountain
highs. They are amazed too.
How can I not love you?

She Is

She is the lipstick on his collar,
The platinum ring around his finger,
Those honest vows of secrecy,
in times of tumultuous mystery.
He runs to her for sheltering sake.
In his mind her well rounded frame is
the epitome of a firm console.
She is made to his liking and fit to mate.
The idea of family she grasp and exhale through
the concepts of her body.
As she aims to please because she is his garden
She keeps the fireplace burning in his heart.
In a moment's notice the world can go hay wire.
But living for one another helps them to
breeze through the changes.
Like colors of red, orange, green and purple.
They learn to become rainbows.
And when they look to the constellation every night.
What a beauty of hope they will share inside.
For love will thrive under the roof of their mouths.
For he strives to make her happy in the wonders of life.
These are the makings of a man with a modern wife.
A real woman's fulfilling dream.

More About The Author and Acknowledgements

Ms. Jessica Hughes
(bka) Jhpoetry and Lipsofmind

https://www.lipsofmind.webs.com
https://www.facebook.com/jh.poetry
email : jhpoetry@gmail.com

Ms. Jessica Hughes has been fortunate enough to attend book signings in various counties. She is eager to participate in another book signing where she currently resides in Charlotte, NC. Jessica participates and enjoys engaging in poetry readings. She also has experience in writing specialized poems for family, friends, and for those who take pleasure in her work. Her poetry has been admired by her peers as well as total strangers. She also has a free ebook currently available titled **"Free Within Poetry"** an anthology written with other distinguished poets. With this being said, the Poetess- Ms. Jessica Hughes would like to say thank you to everyone who has been walking beside her on her poetical journey. She says thank you to those who support her work. And last but, certainly not least, she thanks her Heavenly Father for allowing her to share her gift with everyone around the world.

www.ingramcontent.com/pod-product-compliance
Lightning Source LLC
Chambersburg PA
CBHW020444030426
42337CB00014B/1390